Little Bible Heroes™
The Wise Builder

Written by Victoria Kovacs
Illustrated by Antonio Renna

Nashville TN

GOLDQUILL
WWW.GOLDQUILL.CO.UK

Published by B&H Publishing Group 2019. Text and illustrations copyright © 2019, GoldQuill, United Kingdom.
All rights reserved. Scripture quotations are taken from the Christian Standard Bible®, Copyright © 2017 by Holman Bible Publishers.
Used by permission. Christian Standard Bible® and CSB® are federally registered trademarks of Holman Bible Publishers.
ISBN: 978-1-5359-4265-2   Dewey Decimal Classification: CE
Subject Heading: WISE BUILDER (PARABLE) / THE SOWER (PARABLE) / JESUS CHRIST--PARABLES
Printed in February 2019 in Shenzhen, Guangdong, China
23 22 21 20 19 1 2 3 4 5

Two men build new houses. The wise man builds his house on sturdy rock.

The foolish man
builds his house
on crumbly sand.

It begins to rain.
The rivers flood.
The wild winds blow
against both houses.

The wise man's house doesn't move. It stands on a strong foundation of rock.

But the foolish man's
house falls down.
CRASH! The shifting
sand can't hold it up.

When you don't do what God says, you'll end up like the house built on sand—weak and wobbly.

But when you do what God says, you'll be like the house built on rock— strong and solid!

Remember: "Everyone who hears these words of mine and acts on them will be like a wise man who built his house on the rock."
—Matthew 7:24

Read:
"Blessed are those who hear the word of God and keep it."—Luke 11:28

Think:
1. It is good to listen to what God says in the Bible. Why is it even better to do what He says?

2. What is one thing you can do to obey God today?

Remember:
"If you love me, you will keep my commands."
—John 14:15

Read:

"The seed is the word of God."—Luke 8:11

Think:

1. What can you do to make your heart like the good ground where God's Word can grow?

2. How can you sow or plant God's Word today?

Remember:

"The farmer sows the word."—Mark 4:14 (NIV)

People who hear God's message and do His will are like the good ground where seeds can grow.

Other people let the worries of life act like thorns that keep God's Word from growing in their hearts.

Some people quickly receive God's Word, but when life gets hard and rocky like the road, they forget God's Word.

The seeds are like God's Word. Some people's hearts are like the hard path; they won't listen to God.

But some seeds fall on good soil. These plants grow and make much fruit.

Other seeds fall into thorns.
The thorns choke the plants
so the plants can't grow.

Some seeds fall on rocky ground. The seeds start to grow, but when it gets hot, the sun dries them up.

A farmer goes out to plant seeds.
Some seeds fall along the hard path.
Birds swoop down and gobble them up.

Little Bible Heroes™
The Sower

Written by Victoria Kovacs
Illustrated by Antonio Renna

Published by B&H Publishing Group 2019. Text and illustrations copyright © 2019, GoldQuill, United Kingdom.
All rights reserved. Scripture quotations are taken from the Christian Standard Bible®, Copyright © 2017 by Holman Bible Publishers.
Used by permission. Christian Standard Bible® and CSB® are federally registered trademarks of Holman Bible Publishers.
Scriptures marked NIV are taken from the Holy Bible, New International Version®, NIV® Copyright ©1973, 1978, 1984, 2011 by Biblica, Inc.
Used by permission. All rights reserved worldwide.
ISBN: 978-1-5359-4265-2   Dewey Decimal Classification: CE
Subject Heading: WISE BUILDER (PARABLE) / THE SOWER (PARABLE) / JESUS CHRIST--PARABLES
Printed in February 2019 in Shenzhen, Guangdong, China
23 22 21 20 19 1 2 3 4 5